Bill Gates

The Life, Lessons & Rules For Success

Influential Individuals

Table of Contents

EARLY LIFE – 4

BEGINNINGS IN BUSINESS – 11

THE YOUNG INVENTOR – 19

THE FIRST COMPANY – 25

THE FIRST OF MANY FAILURES – 34

LEGACY – 40

ADVICE FROM THE MAN HIMSELF - 47

PRINCIPLES FOR SUCCESS – 52

50 GREATEST QUOTES – 62

LITTLE KNOWN FACTS - 71

CURRENT DAY - 77

Early Life

Bill Gates is the most influential and recognizable name in the technology industry to date. A business magnate, avid investor, heavy philanthropist, and author of multiple books. Gates and his partner, Paul Allen, together co-founded the technology mogul Microsoft, which quickly grew into the globe's largest PC software company. Gates held different positions at Microsoft over the years, from chief software architect to chairperson and CEO. Up until May 2014, he was also the largest shareholder of the company.

If that is not impressive enough, Gates is currently the richest person in the world with a net worth of over $87 billion. One of his most notable ventures in the latter years of his business ventures has been the partnership he took on with Warren Buffett when they founded The Giving Pledge. This was a cause that encouraged billionaires around the globe to make a pledge promising they would eventually give at least half their entire wealth to philanthropy.

Born in Seattle, Washington to a father who was a very prominent lawyer in the community and a mother who regularly served on the Board of Directors for both United Way and First Interstate BancSystem. Growing up, his parents' dream for him was to practice law like his father. Many people who knew the Gates family a similar view: they were incredibly competitive. Those who grew up and lived alongside the family have always said, no matter what, there was a reward for winning and a penalty for losing. It did not matter if the kids were playing pinball or competing in sports. The only thing that mattered was for every win, there was a reward, and for every loss, a consequence.

This explains a lot behind Gates' eventual wealth and success. He was raised in an environment that outwardly rewarded or penalized every action he made. This makes a child very aware of the decisions they are making and prompts them to learn how to reason and project possible futures based on the current scenario as well as actions taken. This is a skill that he would hone and develop as he grew older, and is argued to be the greatest driving force behind his current success as an adult.

When he was 13, he officially enrolled into his first private prep school. He would end up exploring his first piece of technology that was paid for by the proceeds from a rummage sale the Mother's Club was throwing. They ended up utilizing the profits to purchase a Teletype Model 33 ASR terminal as well as a block of computer time on a General Electric computer. This was to benefit the entire student body as a whole, but obviously certain students took more of an interest than others. Gates was hooked and invested in learning how to program the system. His thirst for knowledge was so great that his math teachers would excuse him from class simply to allow him go and learn the system.

This would be the machine he would write his first piece of code on. The code was an electronic implementation of the traditional tic-tac-toe game that could enable people who used the computer to play against it. Gates would play at every opportunity he got; his school friends soon became entranced with the game. As he watched his fellow student reap the joy from the game he had programmed and loaded onto the computer, he became more and more fascinated with what this piece of technology was capable of doing. He loved how it could always execute the software he programmed perfectly, and he reflects upon this learning experience with only four words: "this machine was neat."

This love of technology would soon lead into his first-ever reprimand on a piece of technology: after the Mother's Club donations had been financially exhausted, Gates and some other students who had struck up similar interests within the piece of technology went to go find alternative time solutions on various systems and minicomputers. Gates and four friends would eventually be banned for an entire summer from the Computer Center Corporation because they were caught finding and exploiting bugs within the main operating systems in order to garner themselves more free computer time.

Eventually CCC finally smartened up and offered the kids an offer they couldn't refuse: they told the children they could have more computer time in exchange for finding bugs within the operating systems and software that CCC's computers utilized. Jumping at the opportunity, Gates found himself going to the CCC's offices and studying their base source codes in order to familiarize himself with back-end knowledge as to how all of their systems worked. The boys would continue to be under this agreement until 1970, when the company went under.

They would not be out of work for long. Information Sciences, Inc. would end up hiring these same four students after hearing of their previous arrangement and technology prowess. Their task? To write a payroll program in a specific coding language. The compensation was not just computer time, however. This time they were also offered royalties, and this would be the first time that Gates would find monetary compensation for his new found passion.

Pretty soon, the administrators above Gates all became aware of his programming capabilities. They would get him to

—

program his own school's electronic classroom assignment software, whereby students could be electronically scheduled for classes they signed up for. Being the young man he was, he ended up utilizing this to his advantage by placing himself in classes that had a vastly large number of "interesting girls" within them.

Gates ended up graduating from his Lakeside Preparatory School in 1973 as a National Merit Scholar, and he ended up only being 10 points underneath a perfect 1600 score when he took the SAT (Scholastic Aptitude Test) required for enrolling into college. In the fall of that graduating year, Gates would enroll into Harvard College and choose pre-law as his major, much to the delight of his parents. He would also end up overloading his schedule to take challenging and time-consuming mathematical classes as well as graduate-level computer science courses, much to the shock of his professors. During his college years at Harvard, Gates took on a series of "unsolved problems," given to his class taught by Harry Lewis. It was a combinatorics class, and the algorithm that Gates devised for pancake sorting was not only correct, but it provided the fastest sorting solution to the problem for over three decades. It was so fast, in fact, that when the successor of the challenge beat Gates' sorting speed solution, it was faster by a mere 1%!

—
8

Even though his major was pre-law, Gates really did not know what he wanted to do with his study plan at Harvard. He spent a great deal of time with the school's computers, and it was during these pre-law college years that him and Paul Allen would begin their own infamous software company. Much to the initial dismay of his parents, when the software company launched Gates dropped out of Harvard in order to pursue his passions. But, while his parents were disappointed in his dropping out, they finally supported him in his technological ventures despite the dreams they might have had for him. Gates did end up giving his parents piece of mind though, striking a deal with Harvard that if this budding technological company did not work out, he would be free to come back and resume his studies without having to officially enroll again.

I guess you could say his "budding technological company" worked out.

Lessons Learned:

- Bill Gates' parents wanted him to be a lawyer, but from a young age he showed incredible programming and technological skills.
- He would eventually drop out of Harvard and take an official leave of absence in order to pursue Microsoft.
- A competitive family home seems to have aided in his eventual success.
- He is another great example of the old adage "follow your passions."

Beginnings in Business

In the beginning, both Gates and Allen were incredibly adventurous with their personal endeavors towards technology. After they read an issue of Popular Electronics at the beginning of 1975, it prompted them to contact Micro Instrumentation and Telemetry Systems, feeding them a lie to gauge potential interest in their skills. The lie? They told MITS that they were developing a BASIC interpreter for the platform that was being utilized on the Altair 8800. The reality of the situation was that they were not, nor had they written any code for it. The actual aim was to gauge their reaction and to weigh the pros and cons of taking on something of that magnitude.

In short, they wanted to know if there was a market.

The response was so positive that the MITS president, Ed Roberts, actually agreed to meet the duo to see a demo of a program they had not yet created. Over the course of a few weeks, they ended up developing an emulator for the Altair that ran on a simple microcomputer. They then utilized that foundation to create the BASIC interpreter for the system. The demonstration was a success and this resulted in a massive deal between the company and the duo in order to distribute the interpreter as Altair BASIC. From this, Paul Allen was hired into MITS and Gates made his leave of absence from Harvard permanent in order to work alongside Allen at MITS in Albuquerque.

This is actually where the term "Microsoft" developed. When they scored their first big partnership with a company, they decided they needed a name for their own partnership. So, they named their partnership "Micro -Soft," and their first office was located in Albuquerque near where they were working for MITS. A year after striking up that partnership and officially naming it, they dropped the hyphen and created the trade name "Microsoft" and officially had it registered in the state of New Mexico. At this point, it became very clear to both Gates and his parents that he was not returning to his studies.

Every rising success story always has its first pitfall. The first technological scandal Gates ever ran into was when he discovered that a copy of Altair BASIC had leaked into the community before it was released officially. It was being copied and widely distributed. At the beginning of 1976, Gates wrote a very open letter to computer hobbyists in the MITS newsletter. It stated, among other things, that more than

90% of the users that were currently utilizing Microsoft Altair BASIC had not actually paid for the product. And by not paying for the product, Gates outlined exactly why it was now in danger of eliminating the very incentive that any professional developer had to create, distribute, and help maintain high-quality software. He stressed that software developers had just as much of a right to demand pay for their work as anyone else in the technological industry.

Out of this scandal, Microsoft ended up becoming independent of MITS later in the year, continuing its development in programming language software for multiple different systems. At the beginning of 1979 they moved operations from Albuquerque, New Mexico to Bellevue, Washington, and never looked back.

During Microsoft's early years Gates saw his responsibility for the budding company flourish. Paul Allen would find his place in the chaos and the first employees would end up having a very broad responsibility for the company's overall business dealings. Gates not only oversaw the business details, but also continued to do what he loved most: write code. Incredibly, Gates personally oversaw and reviewed every single line of code the company ever shipped in the first five years, often rewriting parts as he saw fit before distributing it to customers.

In July 1980, IBM approached Microsoft in regards to a personal computer. The IBM PC that it was about to release to the public. The computer company wanted to sit down and talk with Microsoft about writing an IBM BASIC interpreter that would be unique to their own systems. Not only that, but IBM also expressed interest in developing an operating system alongside Microsoft. The discussions ended up going poorly and they could not reach a unanimous licensing agreement. However, when IBM representative Jack Sam and Bill Gates sat down together to work things out, they would end up coming to an agreement through Gates proposing the 86-DOS operating system. The only issue being that the operating system was very similar to CP/M, the operating system that Seattle Computer Products was already utilizing. Microsoft then had to end up cutting a deal with SCP in order to become the exclusive licensing agent and full owner of 86-DOS. After becoming the full legal owner of that operating system, they were able to adapt it to IBM's personal computer and Microsoft ended up delivering this operating system to the technological company as PC-DOS.

The price? A one-time fee of $50,000.

Smartly, Gates ended up not transferring the copyright onto the operating system. He believed other hardware vendors would try to clone the IBM system and then they would be out of leverage within their own technological market. Because of this, MS-DOS made Microsoft a massive player within their industry, and even though IBM's name was on the operating system, the media quickly pinpointed and identified Microsoft as being "very influential" on this new computer that was taking over the market.

The press was so great and the exposure so loud that their stock rose and demand was huge. This singular event helped spiral them into a restructuring phase that took place in 1981. Gates was not only made president of the company, but also its board chairman.

However, the Microsoft and IBM partnership was not always meant to be. Microsoft ended up launching its first retail version of Microsoft Windows in 1985, striking a deal with IBM in order to develop a separate operating system for their IBM computers. Creative differences at every corner would end up causing great tension between the two companies, with their partnership deteriorating and eventually dissolved beyond repair.

What sets Gates apart from many is that he established his management style very young in Microsoft's years. He was able to bring a massive technological company to fruition whilst being considered distant from others. Many people actually complained that he was never reachable by his phone

---

and rarely returned phone calls. However, that did not mean that he was not hands-on. Gates would meet regularly with the senior and program managers of Microsoft in order to listen to new fresh ideas and proposals. There are many first-hand accounts of these meetings that are drawn on when talking about Gates' management style, with him often being described as verbally combative and constantly berating. At this point he was even considered a risk to the long-term interests of the company.

It turns out this style was for good measure. The whole reasoning behind these outbursts was to get people to defend their proposals in great and utter detail. With such conviction, that Gates would be fully convinced that he could not only implement the proposal, but hire the creator of the proposal to oversee its implementation.

This seemingly verbal abuse in meetings was really Gates vetting whom he was going to hire for specific proposals he decided to take on. If the person could not defend their proposal adequately, then he would not only disregard hiring the person, but would also disregard their proposal as well. Gates understood what he wanted to do and where his place was from an incredibly young age. The inventions he took on and the things he did in high school and post-Harvard solidified his place in the technological industry. The young mogul was not simply a developer of electronics; he was a creator of an entirely new platform that had not yet emerged onto the market.

Gates was a young inventor who was grooming himself to become a lifelong influencer.

Lessons Learned:

- Bill Gates and Paul Allen's first Big Break was based on a lie. Bluffing can occasionally be beneficial if you have the tools to eventually back it up.
- Microsoft and IBM established their official partnership; Gates knew he was no longer returning to Harvard.
- The trademarked name "Microsoft" simply comes from the term that was coined by Gates and Allen when they decided to officially name their partnership.
- Gates had a unique way of managing, but it always seemed to ensure working with the best.
- Even the best companies in the world face pitfalls and challenges.

The Young Inventor

A common misconception about Gates is that he is a serial inventor. On the contrary, he found himself to be exceptionally passionate about and skilled at one particular thing. He capitalized on that one particular facet and made his entire fortune based around it. However, he did have one mishap during his young inventor days. "Traf-O-Data."

If you have not heard of Traf-O-Data, then you are not alone. It was his first company venture with Paul Allen and was a system that was supposed to read and process traffic tapes. The issue was that they never fully got it to work properly and Gates was never able to sell it in order to garner the money necessary to make it work better. The attempt with Paul Allen, who would end up being his co-founder for Microsoft, states that even though Traf-O-Data was not a success, but it was imperative in preparing both him and Gates to create Microsoft's first-ever product that happened a couple of years later.

This traffic counter system they attempted to create was supposed to read raw data from the counters installed on the roadways and generate specific detailed reports for all the traffic engineers in an area. Here is how it was supposed to work: local and state governments frequently do traffic surveys by putting road tubes across the road that cars roll over. This is what establishes the traffic counting system. This black rubber hose that is stretched across the road ends up creating air pulses by the tires that are driven over it which then activates a roadside counter that records it. This tracks not only the number of vehicles that come through a specific area on a daily basis, but it also tracks the speed at which they are coming, even measuring times where there is the most and least traffic on that specific road.

Back during Traf-O-Data's time, the time a car approached as well as the number of axles the car had was punched in by that rubber hose as a 16-bit pattern into a paper tape. Then, cities would hire private companies to come in and translate the data into reports that traffic engineers needed so they could adjust traffic lights and determine how to best improve roads.

If you have ever been traveling down the road and you wonder what this cylindrical black thing is that your tires are about to run over, that is a traffic counter. What Gates and Allen tried to do was to automate the process of extracting this traffic data so it could be cheaper and faster than the local companies being hired privately in order to translate the information. They ended up recruiting their classmates to manually read these hole patterns in the paper tape, and then used those hole patterns to later transcribe the data onto computer cards. Gates would then use a computer to produce traffic flow charts necessary for the traffic engineers.

This was how Traf-O-Data attempted to get its start. However, despite Traf-O-Data's failure, the pair did not give up. Altair BASIC, the software they created for MITS, was their next big adventure. Altair BASIC was so important because the Altair personal computer did not have a screen or a keyboard readily installed onto it, and their basic language program made the machine ultimately easier to use. Not only that, but this was the language they utilized to form the foundation of Microsoft programs they developed up until the creation and generation of MS-DOS.

Coincidentally enough, the next major invention in Gates' career is MS-DOS. This would be the operating system that would serve as the foundation for Windows OS, which would be the system utilized in Windows 98, 99, ME, 2000, and XP. In order to secure purchase for the DOS operating system, however, they did have to contact a company they had previously done business with in order to secure the licensing rights from them. The negotiations went well, and Microsoft would not only make a ton of money off the licensing, but would also make it the standard system for running their specific personal computers.

Gates' inventions were then compounded off this system. He would utilize this to develop the entity of Windows, which would become a dominant graphical user interface that would rival their biggest competitor, Apple Macintosh.

Gates is not just reputable for his invention skills; he is also lauded for his negotiation skills that converted into incredible business deals. When Gates was talking with IBM about the operating system they had developed, he was coming at it the way he did because he wanted to retain the licensing rights to the foundation that would build MS-DOS. In any other circumstance today, that conversation would more than likely have been shut down very quickly without a second thought between the two parties. However, because of Gates' ability to negotiate and swoon, he was able to convince IBM to let him keep the licensing rights to this operating system, and this is what would make Microsoft their fortune.

Gates is not simply an incredible inventor, he is also an incredible software programmer and negotiator. While his first company, Traf-O-Data, did not go as planned, the partnership between him and Allen would bloom into one of the biggest technological companies of all time.

It is this company that gave Gates his fortune.

Lessons Learned:

- He knew what he was good at from a very young age, and he wanted to pursue all those avenues with his friend, Paul Allen.
- Even the best in the world fail sometimes.
- The failure of Traf-O-Data ultimately served to help the duo build their first Microsoft product a couple of years later.
- It is not merely Gates' ability to invent and programme that made him his fortune, but it was also his ability to negotiate.

The First Company

While Traf-O-Data was technically Gates' first official business venture, it also served as his first failure. Traf-O-Data was more valuable to him as a learning tool than as a business, so many attribute Gates' incredible success at Microsoft as also being Gates' "first company."

The Microsoft Corporation is a multinational technology company whose headquarters are located in Redmond, Washington. Microsoft grew to license, develop, create, sell, and support consumer electronics, personal computers, computer software, and all the services that come along with it. To date, the most popular software products are the Microsoft Windows line of operating systems, Internet Explorer, and the Microsoft Office Suite that houses the ever-precious Microsoft Word. However, it also has some hardware products that include the Xbox video game consoles as well as the Microsoft Surface tablet lineup. As if that is not enough, as of 2016 it is the world's largest software maker by revenue as well as one of the globe's most valuable companies.

It is safe to say that Microsoft has been a massive success for Bill Gates.

MS-DOS was created in the mid-1980s, followed quickly by Microsoft Windows. In 1986, Microsoft had their initial public offering where they saw a subsequent rise in their share prices. This drastic rise in share prices created 3 billionaires and around 12,000 millionaires among all of the Microsoft employees who were holding shares as business perks for being employed with the company.

Since the 1990s, Microsoft has worked diligently to diversify themselves among the operating system market, and during that pursuit, a number of corporate acquisitions have been made. In 2011, Microsoft ended up acquiring Skype and the technologies that surrounded for $8.5 billion. At the end of 2016, Microsoft added to the portfolio and ended up purchasing LinkedIn for $26 billion.

Over the years Microsoft didn't branch out to create its own line of personal computers and simply stuck with engineering and creating the software for these systems. Up until 2012 that is. In 2012, Microsoft officially entered the personal computer production market for the very first time and launched the Microsoft Surface, which was a line of tablet computers. Not too long after, Microsoft acquired smartphone software and introduced themselves into the smartphone hardware market.

They acquired Nokia's devices and services and ended up forming Microsoft Mobile as a result, founded in the confidence the company harnessed from their successful launch of the Surface tablet.

With all the success Microsoft has seen, it is no wonder that people are always clamoring to know how it started. Paul Allen and Bill Gates officially established Microsoft on April 4th, 1975 during their partnership with MITS. The duo decided to name Gates as the CEO in the beginning, and Paul Allen is the one who is attributed to giving it the original name of "Micro-Soft." A couple of years after they officially declared themselves a company, in August of 1977, the newly-budding company formed an agreement with ASCII magazine based out of Japan. This is important because it resulted in the very first international office Microsoft would ever have, entitled ASCII Microsoft.

When the 1980s turned a corner, Microsoft entered the OS business with its own version of Unix. They called it Xenix, and it was popular in its own right. However, MS-DOS was so popular that this was the platform that would solidify the company's dominance in the market in the 1980s. It is this dominance that would set them on the path to harnessing the licensing capabilities for this product, and it is this ability to license the product that would make Microsoft the leading personal computer operating systems vendor.

During this time of exploration, Microsoft wanted to attempt expanding into new markets. They released the Microsoft Mouse in 1983 as well as a publishing division entitled Microsoft Press. But, during all of these new ventures, Paul Allen would step down from Microsoft after developing Hodgkin's disease, much to Gates' dismay and worry. Microsoft would coast in its revenue acquisitions, allowing their company to ride out these new ventures and see what would come of them until the 1990s. The 1990s would bring about a great deal of legal heartache for Gates and Microsoft. Due to their partnership with IBM, the Federal Trade Commission would sink their teeth into Microsoft for possible collusion against IBM. This would mark the beginning of a decade's worth of legal clashes between Microsoft and the U.S. government that would eventually end with all parties wanting the nightmare to end. The case quickly turned into a game of he-said-she-said, with IBM determined to prove that Microsoft was colluding with competitors in order to bump them out of the game. Microsoft was making the same complaint against IBM.

Many different factors went into the investigation the U.S. government conducted into the IBM/Microsoft partnership-collusion issue. One of the issues that rose was Microsoft's dominating and almost-monopoly market on the operating system software that many personal computers utilized. There were other accusations made, such as the fact that Microsoft integrating Internet Explorer into its software was their version of stealing intellectual property from IBM's attempts to integrate Netscape into its personal computers. In the end, the courts did not seek to break up Microsoft in any fashion, they found them not guilty of any monopoly-like state or collusion, and they merely wanted to find a resolution to the antitrust case as quickly as possible.

After this hiccup in Microsoft's history, the company continued to see valuable gains. As the 90s waned on, Microsoft began to redefine its product line once again and expanded its offerings into the computer networking arena as well as the World Wide Web. Due to this expansion, the company released Windows 95. This featured a pre-emptive multitasking capability, which was a completely new interface that had a novel "start" button. Not only that, 32-bit capabilities also came bundled with an online service since Microsoft had been found not in violation of any intellectual property rights.

For those of you that remember MSN, that was the bundled online service it first offered.

Soon after, in 1996, Microsoft would branch itself out again into new territories. Microsoft reached out to NBC Universal to create a 24/7-cable news station, entitled MSNBC. If you have ever wondered where the infamous idea for 24/7 cable news stations came from, you can thank Microsoft for it. Microsoft would find itself entrenched once again in legal problems in October of 1997, when the U.S. Justice Department filed a motion with many federal district courts. Their motion stated that the company violated an agreement that was signed in 1994 after the previous scandal had been wrapped up, stating that this supposed agreement prohibited the company from bundling any type of internet interface with their Windows products. In the motion they asked Microsoft to stop bundling Internet Explorer with their Windows products.

Bill Gates and the company was no longer a stranger to these types of court cases. With the mounting responsibility of a company such as Microsoft comes the mounting responsibility to defend it when people want to question it. All in all, Microsoft saw large gains, continued accomplishments, and constantly led the frontier in not only the operating systems front, but the media front as well.

Various companies banded together and ended up forming The Trusted Computing platform Alliance in October of 1999. This was in order to protect intellectual property and increase intellectual properties' security by identifying changes in hardware and software on a base code level. Many of the critics of this alliance, just like the critics of Gates' letter he wrote to the people of MITS when his software was being illegally distributed, cried out that this was a way to enforce indiscriminate restrictions on how every single consumer would utilize their software, which would give the alliance potential access to rule how a personal computer behaved. For critics, they saw an example scenario where a computer was not only secured for the owner, but was also secured against the owner.

As in, it was their device, but not really their device.

On April 3rd, 2000, a judgment would be handed down in the case of United States v. Microsoft, which would end up calling the company an abusive monopoly.

Despite the various pitfalls in Microsoft's history, no one can deny that Microsoft was a pioneering frontier leader of technological capacities. These court cases served as learning tools for Bill Gates, He would find that the company's reputation for quality products that he had worked and striven so hard to build would supersede any ruling these court cases brought down upon the company's head. On January 13th, 2000, Bill Gates would hand over his CEO position to Steve Ballmer, his old college friend from his

Harvard days. Utilizing his newfound time to pursue other philanthropic passions.

With Gates' story, there is much to be learned through his failures as there are in his successes.

Lessons Learned:

- Microsoft had several court cases brought against it for various reasons surrounding becoming a monopoly.
- To become one of the biggest companies in the world, it is impossible not to step on a few toes in the process.
- Monopoly or not, Microsoft offered huge value to the market which will always attract customers.
- Microsoft continually branched into markets that garnered popularity, but had not yet garnered substance. This is why Microsoft excelled greatly in many of the ventures it took on outside the operating systems market.

The First Of Many Failures

While Traf-O-Data might be Gates' most "popular" failure, it taught both him and Allen a great deal of lessons in the idea of market research. Time and time again, Paul Allen admits their business plan for the failed traffic information company was flawed, and the fact that they did not bother to do any market research only enhanced their failures. In the few years Traf-O-Data was up and running, it lost over $3,000.00 in net profits, forcing the two to shut the doors on their first-ever business venture together.

But, that is not the only failure Bill Gates would encounter during his career. Failure is a key component of success and should be studied due to the lessons it provides. Through learning from the failures of others, we can spot common trends and avoid common pitfalls ourselves. It also shows us that even the geniuses of this world will make their errors along the way.

Another failure that many business analyses experts feel Gates made was the fact that he did not engage the government early through the development of a company that would have such an impact on the world. After taking Microsoft from a mere two-man startup all the way to the tech juggernaut it is today, many people believe that Gates did not engage the government nearly enough in the process of Microsoft's rise. When Microsoft's competitors were lobbying the government, Gates' attitude was that the government should just leave them alone. Brad Silverberg, who spent nine years as Microsoft's Senior Vice President, has frequently stated he felt this was a massive mistake on Gates' part.

Through Gates' eyes, the company was competing fairly even though it was competing hard. He felt he was creating value for his customers through enhancing their lives, and that should have been enough. Silverberg, and many other business analysts, tribute the U.S. government's attack on Microsoft that resulted in all those court cases to the fact that Microsoft was not lobbying their points to the government. Microsoft paid a devastating price, both within the media and monetarily. Many people felt it could have been avoided. Gates is notably known for the work he does philanthropically through the Bill and Melinda Gates Foundation. One of the many things they attempted to tackle was working to reduce the size of classrooms in public schools across the nation. However, the foundation also supported Common Core Curriculum standards within this attempt at public school reform. This would prove to be a massive downfall for the foundation, and it cost them a great deal of resources and money in the process. The Foundation greatly underestimated the resources and support that would be required to well-equip educators and implement the standards necessary not only to reduce classroom size, but to also implement this type of curriculum. They missed an opportunity to engage the educators and teachers of this country's children, and they also missed an incredible opportunity to immerse the parents and communities in the children's education so that the benefits of this particular standard could have succeeded from the beginning.

Whilst CEO of Microsoft, Gates could be accused of lacking in response to the opportunity and threat of the Internet. Because Windows in the late 90s was so successful, Gates was focused on protecting Windows and not protecting the company's business and system strategy, and this is what eventually led to Microsoft's position decline come the turn of the millennia. But, it seems as if the company is now coming to terms with the new reality stemming from the Internet, and it seems to be making necessary changes that is climbing Microsoft back up the charts.

Gates also ignored search engines. In his own words, Google kicked their butts. Larry Page and Sergey Brin launched their little company known as Google in 1998, and around the same time Gates introduced his own search engine called MSN Search. The little-known Google startup would end up besting the tech giant because Google was not only innovative and fast, it also delivered relevant results. MSN Search had none of the above, and to make matters worse, Microsoft had not even bothered to develop their own algorithm for their own search engine. They simply used search results from an existing search engine called Inktomi.

The truth of the matter was that Search was not a priority for Gates or Microsoft at the time. The company had been focusing solely on the success of Windows, and Google ended up surpassing them by a long way. This would put Microsoft second or even third best to Google ever since.

Arguably the biggest mistake Gates made was funding his competition. As a result of the antitrust suit that Microsoft experienced against IBM, they found themselves at a standstill. Apple agreed to drop their part of the lawsuit in exchange for Microsoft purchasing non-voting shares of stock and supporting Office for the Mac for five years. This was a negotiated deal that took place behind closed doors, and it resulted in Gates filtering a lot of money through Apple's doors early on in the company. Apple was also one of the companies that had complained of Microsoft stealing intellectual property from them. The back-door negotiations went well, resulting in Apple dropping their portion of the lawsuit. Dropping the lawsuit would then create a cascading effect that would finally bring an end to the antitrust lawsuits. In the end, Microsoft ended up purchasing $150 million in non-voting options stocks, giving Apple the funding needed in order to get its fledgling company off the ground. Unknowingly aiding a company that would become Microsoft's biggest rival in the process.

Even the richest and arguably most successful person the world has ever seen has made his fair share of mistakes. In the words of the man himself, "Success is a lousy teacher. It seduces smart people into thinking they cannot lose."

Lessons Learned:

- Failures and mistakes are inevitable to all, learn and adapt from them.

Legacy

For a man such as Bill Gates, it has hard to pinpoint a moment that epitomizes the start of what would become his most important work. The true lasting legacy he will leave behind. It could be argued that point of no return was when he officially made the decision not to return to Harvard. When he and Paul Allen were working with MITS while they were still in school, the first major deal they did with the company resulted in Gates taking a leave of absence from Harvard. He had discussed it with his teachers and the Admissions Office and came to an agreement that if his business venture did not work out, he could come back to school without having to re-enroll and pick up where he left off. Then, when him and Allen officially named their partnership and did their first successful deal with MITS, he made his dropout from Harvard official.

There are some that believe the turning point in Gates' career is when he was able to successfully obtain the licensing for MS-DOS. He had to jump through a substantial amount of hoops and do a great deal of verbal seducing and negotiating in order to get all parties involved to agree to what was going on. In order for him to give IBM the operating system they were wanting, he had to go back to a prior company that Microsoft had worked with and convince them to hand over the rights to the material they had created for them. Even though he had created the operating system for the other company, they held intellectual rights, and he had to get those back. It was Gates smooth-talking that convinced this other company to give him back the licensing rights to the operating system so he could deliver the newly-developed operating system IBM was wanting. After that, it became a matter of convincing IBM to still take the operating system that had been created without taking the licensing rights along with it. When he convinced both companies to forgo licensing rights to what would become MS-DOS, he would utilize that licensing agreement in order to put Microsoft on the map. However, there was another turning point in his life that came later after he left Microsoft that has a strong case for being the moment that sparked the beginning of Gates' most important work. When he finally stepped down from the company in the early 2000s, him and his wife, Melinda Gates, started their philanthropic journey: The Bill and Melinda Gates foundation. After starting the foundation, the first major moment came on the couple's first trip to Africa. This turning point would not only solidify the idea of opening the foundation, it would solidify the beginning of his role as one of the leading figures in philanthropy worldwide.

During this trip, the pair had their first encounter with severe poverty. They were watching families struggle to feed their newborns, even witnessing children die in the hands of helpless parents. For the Gates couple, it was a heartbreaking trip.

Post-trip, the couple took up an extensive amount of reading and research, only to find that millions of children in Africa were dying from diseases the US no longer experiences. Diseases such as yellow fever, measles, and rotavirus were killing half a million kids every year throughout the country, and this was mortifying to Bill and Melinda.

To Gates, this was simply unacceptable. He understood he was lucky to never have heard of some of these diseases because of the privilege this nation experiences with its health and medical system, but he was appalled when he realized there was no extensive worldwide effort to save these children from their deaths. That first trip to Africa would be the first in a long line of trips both him and his wife would take in order to learn, help, and garner more information to bring back with them to the Foundation. To him, there was no substitute for going and seeing for himself what was happening to these children on a daily basis.

When asked to define philanthropy, Gates says the role of philanthropy is to "get things started." They utilized the Foundation and its funds to set up a basic system to make the market forces of the US work in favor of the poor. This meant guaranteeing purchases so drug companies could make some money in order to invest in the wellbeing of the less-privileged. While many do not understand this to be a good thing, it ended up having some incredible incentives: when the value of approaching the markets in this way became clear, many governments ended up putting their own money into the world market to add to these incentives. This is what would prompt drug companies to begin factoring poor-world diseases into their business model, thus sparking a massive philanthropic call across the world to help these countries in need.

In essence, because of Gates and the incentive plan for the world market he started, drug companies and businesses were prompted to run by the moral code he was hoping to instill. The truth of the matter is that most first world people, even Bill Gates, take for granted the fact that children in the US will not die in droves from particular diseases like malaria or polio. However, when Gates took that first fateful trip to Africa, he came face-to-face with the fact that this is not true for every parent in the world. It was an eye-opener. It was an experience he had taken on with his wife that would be forever seared into his mind. He states that anyone can help with these efforts, whether you invest your time to volunteer or donate money to a charity. He understands that philanthropy is not just for the millionaires and billionaires of the world, it is a moral code that we are all able to take on. Launched in 2000, the foundation is the largest transparently operated private foundation in the world. The primary aims of the foundation worldwide are to reduce extreme poverty and enhance healthcare. In America, the foundation aims to increase access to information technology and educational opportunities. Recent records show an endowment of $44.3 billion. Due to the methodology of applying business techniques to the way of receiving donations makes it one of the leaders in venture philanthropy. Gates has pledged an estimated $28 billion of his own money with fellow billionaire Warren Buffett also donating a significant sum. The decision was also made that once the couple pass away, 98% of their net worth will be donated to the foundation with all funding being used within 20 years. This is to ensure the bulk of the money will be put towards charitable causes and not slowly frittered away over a long period of time on administration costs and salaries.

Philanthropy has proven to be the most rewarding job Gates has had. He boasts that it is just as thrilling as it is humbling, and that he knew this was something he was born to do: raise awareness, get things started, and ingrain in others the need to look out for the less fortunate in this world.

Lessons Learned:

- There can be no denying the legacy Gates will leave behind due to both his technological and philanthropic work.
- The lessons he learned in business have transferred over well in aiding him with his foundation.
- The world is a much better place due to Bill Gates.

Advice From The Man Himself

Bill Gates recently took to social media feeds in order to give the recent batch of college graduates a bit of advice. Gates is widely sought out among millennial youth of the more recent generations not simply because of the success he has garnered, but because of the philanthropic notions and movements he has contributed to societies around the world. He gave these recent college graduates four specific points to think about, but they can apply to any person of any age.

The first tip was a suggestion into the three specific industries that are currently in high demand with exciting prospects for the future. Energy, the biosciences, and artificial intelligence are the three fields that Gates believes have great potential not only for long-term careers, but also for entrepreneurial benefits. The reasoning? Areas like technology and science are only expected to grow over the next several years. Gates stated that people who have backgrounds in these three sectors will be the most in-demand employees in the next two decades. He even went so far as to state that if he were starting out in this day and age, these would be the three sectors he would consider for his own college career.

The second piece of advice he gave in his social media-based advice share was to choose one's relationships wisely. It is no secret that Warren Buffett and Bill Gates have been friends for many years, and Gates wholly believes that his friendship with this legendary American magnate and investor that has substantially aided his career and personal qualities. Both Gates and Buffett have stated that those whom you keep in your inner social circle will not only impact your work life, but your personal life as well. Gates says to indulge and surround oneself with people who challenge, teach, and push an individual to be the best version of themselves they can possibly be. Gates also made a statement about encouraging the younger generations to make smart romantic choices. After all, whom you marry is going to be a huge influence towards your life and the type of person you will become.

His philanthropic side came to rise in the third point he made, which was encouraging individuals to educate themselves on the world's problems. He states within this listed point that one of his biggest personal regrets was that he did not learn more about the world's problems and the global inequality that swallows many countries until much later in his life. He states that being more aware of the problems humanity as a whole faces will make someone better equipped to solve them in the long run, as well as incorporate them into one's moral code and any business model an entrepreneur might develop. His last point made is aimed at everyone no matter your situation: he told everyone to stay energized. Simply put, he stated that it was one of the most incredible times any individual could be alive, and that he wanted to make sure everyone made the most of it. Stay energized and take it all in. But, above all else, what we can learn from Gates' career is that valuing your time is essential. An infamous Gates quote fits wonderfully here: "no matter how much money you have, you can't buy more time." Gates consistently understood the importance of time management and utilizing it wisely in the days you have, and he would always make sure to prioritize his tasks from what mattered most to what mattered least to him. He did not organize them in an order based upon what made him the most money, but he organized them in terms of what would impact himself and his business the most. If he did not believe he needed to be in a meeting, then he was simply not at that meeting. On the flip side, if he took the time to communicate with someone that was closest to him and he realized he was needed somewhere in his personal life, he would make sure to always make the time to fulfill that specific commitment. This aspect is what would help him balance his business life with his personal life; it is what

---

49

would keep his marriage with his wife flourishing when many businessmen find themselves drowning in divorce settlements.

What is interesting throughout all of this is the range of personal advice that comes from someone who is a businessman. It shows us that business is not merely about business, but that it has a personal aspect that needs to be nurtured, respected, and attended to properly. Removing the personal aspect from a business diminishes passion, stunts vision, and disables an individual from projecting towards the future.

Lessons Learned:

- Bill Gates states that his biggest personal regret is not learning about global poverty and indecencies that plague many countries sooner in his life.
- He took to social media this year during college graduations and gave many millennial graduates advice on where to go from here, including staying energized and focusing on the sciences, energy, and artificial intelligence industries.
- His philanthropic aspirations show us that, even though business is important, people still have a responsibility towards the world around us.
- Managing your time effectively is key.

Principles For Success

People of all ages and every industry have been eating up whatever this man has recommended for decades, and rightly so. This is a list of the greatest lessons I believe Bill Gates has shared with the world. The principles are timeless and can be incorporated into your own life today. On pursuit of improvement, it is wise to learn from the best.

Extraordinary focus

During HBO's new documentary Becoming Warren Buffett, there is a scene with Bill Gates. Whilst Buffett and Gates are sitting together at a table, both men were asked to write on a piece of paper the one thing they felt had contributed most to their success. Sure enough, both men had unknowingly written down the same word: focus. It surely can't be a coincidence that two of the most successful men of this era chose the same answer, only further highlighting the importance of complete focus to achieving great success.

Enjoy what you do

To get the best out of someone, Gates states that person needs to enjoy whatever it is they're doing. He was absorbed in solving the technological problems he would encounter whilst coding. It was one of the reasons he was able to devote so many hours of his life towards a task many others would see as boring.

Get lucky

With an estimated I.Q of 160 and the creation of one of the most successful companies in the world, Gates is obviously a very smart man. Often not mentioned is how he has also benefitted from a fair amount of dumb luck. He began his obsession with computers whilst at middle school in 1968, spending countless hours learning how to program. Here's where the dumb luck comes in: in the 1960s, very few colleges had computer labs and a middle school with a computer was unheard of. The chances of a 13-year-old having access to a computer were pretty much one-in-a-million.

Utilize the luck you're given

Gates obviously had his slice of luck, but having access to computers was only the start. He dedicated himself completely to becoming the best programmer he could be, often having to be kicked out of the computer room as he was spending so much time there. It was through these hours upon hours of practice that ultimately led to him possessing the skills to start Microsoft. Each of us has our own unique opportunities surrounding us. Take in your luck for a moment – and then capitalize on it.

Create the future you wish to see

Bill Gates has described his imagination and foresight as one of the greatest assets to achieving business success. He developed new technology and designed new opportunities due in large part to the creative thinking aspect of engineering. Where is the world of technology going? How can we create and innovate existing concepts? How do people imagine the future regarding a certain medium? Whatever the industry, dreaming up the future is the first step towards seeing it realized. Creating something that solves a problem, fills a need or engineers innovative solutions begins with making the transition from creative thought to applied principles.

Minimize procrastination

Gates had to resolve this flaw in himself. It was something he suffered with whilst at Harvard. Many of us suffer from procrastination issues as we all think we may have more time or energy to complete a task than we do. Bill Gates frequently discussed the need to break bad habits in order to ensure the proper function of a business. It is wise to self assess any bad habits that cause procrastination that you may need to break.

Bite off more than you can chew

Microsoft's big break came from a lie Bill Gates told the computer company MITS as mentioned previously. When asked to present this software they hadn't yet created, it forced Gates to put everything he had into creating before the presentation date. He made the sale, and one month later Microsoft was officially founded.

By always pushing yourself to deliver a little bit more than you've proven yourself capable of, you'll go further and faster in your business ventures. That being said, actually lying to potential clients is probably not advisable!

Quality is crucial

Microsoft grew fast. As it took on more and more programmers, Gates became busier with CEO duties that no longer called for programming. That didn't stop him from reviewing – and often rewriting – every single line of code that the company released.

Gates' keen eye for detail ensured that Microsoft always produced quality software. It also made sure that he never lost track of his team and the work they were producing.

As a business grows and new employees are hired, it may be tempting to just let them work and trust that they're doing a good job. But companies have a reputation to protect, so it is wise to take a page from Gates' book by keeping a close watch on a team's output.

Lead the trail

At one point, computer screens displayed just text. In the early 80's, Bill Gates and Steve Ballmer would travel around the country delivering seminars about how graphic interfaces were the operating systems of the future – but nobody believed them.

The general response was that graphic interfaces would be too slow and that it would be difficult to write the correct software for them. They were pessimistic on the outcome when Microsoft announced in 1983 that it was developing Windows.

Attitudes soon changed in 1984, when Apple launched the Macintosh. It became the first commercially successful computer with a graphical user interface. It was now obvious to everyone that the future involved windows, icons, menus, and a pointing device. Soon after, the market was flooded with graphical OS software. Notable examples include Workbench, Deskmate and – of course – Microsoft Windows. Microsoft was able to release Windows 1.0 in 1985, just one year after the Mac's success. This was because they had actually started developing the software two years earlier. If you've got a revolutionary idea that you truly believe in, don't worry if other people don't get it. Start developing it now so that you'll be prepared when the time is right.

Share your vision with your team

By May 1995, Gates was convinced that the Internet was Microsoft's future. He wanted to ensure his team followed his vision so wrote his thoughts and beliefs on a memo to all employees. It concluded with:

"The Internet is a tidal wave. It changes the rules. It is an incredible opportunity as well as incredible challenge. I am looking forward to your input on how we can improve our strategy to continue our track record of incredible success." Gates realized how important the Internet would become and this memo made sure his team knew too. As a result, Windows 95 came bundled with Internet Explorer. By spelling out your aims to your team in a clear and concise way, a more coherent group effort is nearly guaranteed to follow.

Play bridge

Gates advises everyone get into a mix of strategic and competitive games as pastime activities and loves to play bridge. His theory being that competitive gaming that keeps the mind fresh and a competitive spirit close to hand will ultimately help in the world of business. Bridge is also fellow billionaire Warren Buffett's favorite game. Now I'm not promising taking up bridge will make you a billionaire like those two, but it will improve your decision making in general.

Learn from unhappy customers

Bill Gates has millions of happy customers, but also a fair share of unhappy customers. Anyone who has had the experience of staring at the "blue screen of death" understands why.

But as much as people love to complain about Windows, it is still the market leader. Windows has been the world's primary desktop operating system since 1990 and it currently boasts a tidy 84.31% market share as of June 2017.

The reason is simple: Microsoft continues to listen to customer feedback and improve their products. Gates stated it best himself: "Your most unhappy customers are your greatest source of learning."

Surround yourself with good people

Gates realized early on the necessity of hiring trustworthy, hard-working, bright individuals. Having an assurance that those close to you are on your side, there to help and possess the specific needed skill set that compliment your vision are all vital to success.

Know when to ask for help

Following on from the last point, Gates also knows his limitations. It is impossible to be excellent at everything. He wasn't afraid to take advice in the areas he wasn't great at. He also stated that surrounding yourself with people who are smarter than you will provide more opportunities to learn and work together on the path to creating a successful business venture.

Perseverance

Unknown to many, Windows 1.0 wasn't much of a success. In 1987, along came Windows 2.0 but it didn't fare much better. It found moderate success thanks to certain software –

in particular, Excel, Word, and Aldus Pagemaker.

It wasn't until 1990, when Microsoft launched Windows 3.0, that they found significant success with a graphical operating system. It was a big moneymaker for the company and it sold over 10 million units in just two years. Microsoft had found the model that would be the start of the computer software giant we know today. If you have complete belief in your idea, often perseverance can be the difference between success and failure. Adapt, improve and keep at it.

50 Greatest Quotes

"Patience is a key element of success."

"Success is a lousy teacher. It seduces smart people into thinking they can't lose."

"It's fine to celebrate success, but it is more important to heed the lessons of failure."

"People always fear change. People feared electricity when it was invented, didn't they?"

"If you can't make it good, at least make it look good."

"I have been struck again and again by how important measurement is to improving the human condition."

"If I'd had some set idea of a finish line, don't you think I would have crossed it years ago?"

"We always overestimate the change that will occur in the next two years and underestimate the change that will occur in the next ten. Don't let yourself be lulled into inaction."

"To win big, you sometimes have to take big risks."

"We've got to put a lot of money into changing behavior."

"Of my mental cycles, I devote maybe 10% to business thinking. Business isn't that complicated. I wouldn't want that on my business card."

"I choose a lazy person to do a hard job. Because a lazy person will find an easy way to do it."

"Television is not real life. In real life people actually have to leave the coffee shop and go to jobs."

"Life is not fair – get used to it!"

"If geek means you're willing to study things, and if you think science and engineering matter, I plead guilty. If your culture doesn't like geeks, you are in real trouble."

"Don't compare yourself with anyone in this world. If you do so, you are insulting yourself."

"As we look ahead into the next century, leaders will be those who empower others."

" 'I don't know' has become 'I don't know yet'."

"I really had a lot of dreams when I was a kid, and I think a great deal of that grew out of the fact that I had a chance to read a lot."

"Your most unhappy customers are your greatest source of learning."

"Flipping burgers is not beneath your dignity. Your Grandparents had a different word for burger flipping – they called it opportunity."

"Our success has really been based on partnerships from the very beginning."

"This is a fantastic time to be entering the business world, because business is going to change more in the next 10 years than it has in the last 50."

"The world won't care about your self-esteem. The world will expect you to accomplish something BEFORE you feel good about yourself."

"If you think your teacher is tough, wait till you get a boss."

"Expectations are a form of first-class truth: If people believe it, it's true."

"We all need people who will give us feedback. That's how we improve."

"Intellectual property has the shelf life of a banana."

"The first rule of any technology used in a business is that automation applied to an efficient operation will magnify the efficiency. The second is that automation applied to an inefficient operation will magnify the inefficiency."

"Everyone needs a coach. It doesn't matter whether you're a basketball player, a tennis player, a gymnast, or a bridge player."

"In business, the idea of measuring what you are doing, picking the measurements that count, like customer satisfaction and performance ... you thrive on that."

"[Intelligence is] an elusive concept. There's a certain sharpness, an ability to absorb new facts. To walk into a situation, have something explained to you and immediately say, "Well, what about this?" To ask an insightful question. To absorb it in real time. A capacity to remember. To relate to

domains that may not seem connected at first. A certain creativity that allows people to be effective"

"Don't make the same decision twice. Spend time and thought to make a solid decision the first time so that you don't revisit the issue unnecessarily. If you're too willing to reopen issues, it interferes not only with your execution but also with your motivation to make a decision in the first place. After all, why bother deciding an issue if it isn't really decided?"

"Information technology and business are becoming inextricably interwoven. I don't think anybody can talk meaningfully about one without talking about the other."

"If I had to say what is the thing that I feel best about, it's being involved in this whole software revolution and what comes out of that, because you can go all over the world and go into schools and see these computers being used and go into hospitals and see them being used, and see how they're tools for sharing information that hopefully

---

leads to more peaceful conditions, and just the great research advances that come out of that."

"If you show people the problems and you show people the solutions, they will be moved to act."

"Whether it's Google or Apple or free software, we've got some fantastic competitors and it keeps us on our toes."

"A bad strategy will fail no matter how good your information is, and lame execution will stymie a good strategy. If you do enough things poorly, you will go out of business."

"Business people need to shake off the notion that information is hard to get."

"Only a few businesses will succeed by having the lowest price, so most will need a strategy that includes customer services."

"Customers want high quality at low prices and they want it now."

"A company's ability to respond to an unplanned event, good or bad, is a prime indicator of its ability to compete."

"Reward worthy failure - experimentation."

"Treatment without prevention is simply unsustainable"

"Eradications are special. Zero is a magic number. You either do what it takes to get to zero and you're glad you did it; or you get close, give up and it goes back to where it was before, in which case you wasted all that credibility, activity, money that could have been applied to other things."

"When you want to do your homework, fill out your tax return, or see all the choices for a trip you want to take, you need a full-size screen."

"Who decides what's in Windows? The customers who buy it."

"I never took a day off in my twenties. Not one."

"Steve Jobs' ability to focus in on a few things that count, get people who get user interface right, and market things as revolutionary are amazing things."

"Like my friend Warren Buffett, I feel particularly lucky to do something every day that I love to do. He calls it 'tap-dancing to work.'"

"We make the future sustainable when we invest in the poor, not when we insist on their suffering."

Little Known Facts

Most people think of three things when Bill Gates comes to mind:

1.   He's the richest man in the world.

2.   He co-founded one of the most successful tech companies of all time.

3.   He's an extremely generous philanthropist through his foundation.

Aside from these three things, as can be expected there is far more to the man. Here I've compiled a list of twenty facts not so widely known.

#1 Gates originally aimed to become a millionaire by the age of 30, he became a billionaire at 31

#2 If Bill Gates was a country he would be the #63 richest on earth.

#3 His biggest regret in life so far? The fact that he doesn't know any foreign languages.

#4 As a teenager, gates read the entire "world book encyclopedia" series from start to finish.

#5 Two years after he dropped out of Harvard, Gates was arrested in New Mexico. He was driving without a license and ran a red light. If you've ever seen the infamous mug shot photo of gates as a youngster, this was the reason.

#6 Speaking of cars, Gates has quite the Porsche collection. The headliner is his Porsche 959 sports car, which he bought 13 years before the car was approved by the epa or department of transportation. I can confirm he now has a license.

#7 At Microsoft, gates used to memorize employees' license plates to keep tabs on their comings and goings. "eventually I had to loosen up, as the company got to a reasonable size," he said.

#8 Alongside fellow billionaire Warren Buffett, Gates has a McDonald's gold CARD THAT provides unlimited free fast food from the place.

#9 For air travel, gates used to fly coach. He now gets around in the plane he's owned since 1997, when his net worth was already 36 billion. He calls this purchase his "big splurge."

#10 Bill gates has saved 6 million lives through his foundation providing vaccines and better healthcare.

#11 Besides his plane, one of Gates biggest splurges was the codex leicester, a collection of writings by Leonardo Da Vinci. He acquired the codex at a 1994 auction for $30.8 million.

#12 Even at his fortune's peak, gates was only the 6th richest man of all time when adjusted for inflation.

#13 Despite his immense wealth, Gates says his kids will only inherit $10 million each — just a fraction of his $87 billion net worth. "leaving kids massive amounts of money is not a favor to them," he says.

#14 When Steve Jobs was dying, Gates wrote him a letter. Jobs kept it beside his bed until the end.

#15 Gates says if Microsoft hadn't worked out, he probably would've been a researcher for artificial intelligence.

#16 Gates predicted (very inaccurately) in 2004 that within two years, email spam would have disappeared.

#17 Queen Elizabeth of England knighted Gates with the KBE order in 2005, in recognition of his charitable contributions worldwide.

#18 Gates earned an honorary degree from Harvard in 2007, thirty-two years after dropping out. His commencement speech is available on YouTube.

#19 Gates says he reads 50 books a year, stating "reading is still the main way that I both learn new things and test my understanding."

#20 What's left on gates' bucket list? Just don't die.

Current Day

Gates currently resides in a 66,000-Sq. Ft. mansion in Washington that cost an estimated $500 million to build. With the foundation still flourishing, there is a good chance that Gates and his wife, Melinda, will spend the rest of their lives working in philanthropy and growing their Foundation. But, it seems he will never be able to completely step away from Microsoft. In 2014, after the newly appointed CEO Satya Nadella took over his position, he took on the role of Technology Advisor in order to support the transition. He has stated that he will help alongside Nadella to forward the new CEO's strategic vision, and that he will help the reorganization of his company solidified before truly stepping down.

However, his stepping down remains to be seen, and his philanthropic efforts are stronger than ever. The foundation's most recent contribution to date was a three-year award for over $3 million to Aryeh D. Stein, PhD, MPH. To be used in order to support and fund his research into examining the role that childhood development and socio-economic status had on a person's socio-emotional and cognitive functioning as they grow into their adulthood years. The Gates Foundation is now well into tackling problems within their own country. From the failure of Traf-O-Data to changing the world forever with Microsoft, all the way to establishing the wealthiest philanthropic entity the world has ever seen. When Bill Gates sets his mind to something, he determines to do it to the best of his ability. The lessons we can pull from his career and the morals we can pull from his established foundation are essential to those growing up in an era where entrepreneurship has boomed and the education of worldviews and politics has become paramount.

Whether Gates steps away from his company or whether he continues his philanthropic efforts until the day he passes, there is only one thing that is near on certain:

Bill Gates is not done making his mark just yet.

Thanks for checking out my book. I hope you found this of value and enjoyed it. If this was the case, head to my author page for more like this. Before you go, I have one small favor to ask…

Would you take 60 seconds and write a quick blurb about this book on Amazon?

Reviews are the best way for independent authors (like me) to get noticed, sell more books, and it gives me the motivation to continue producing. I also read every review and use the feedback to write future revisions – and even future books. Thanks again.

Made in the USA
Lexington, KY
26 May 2019